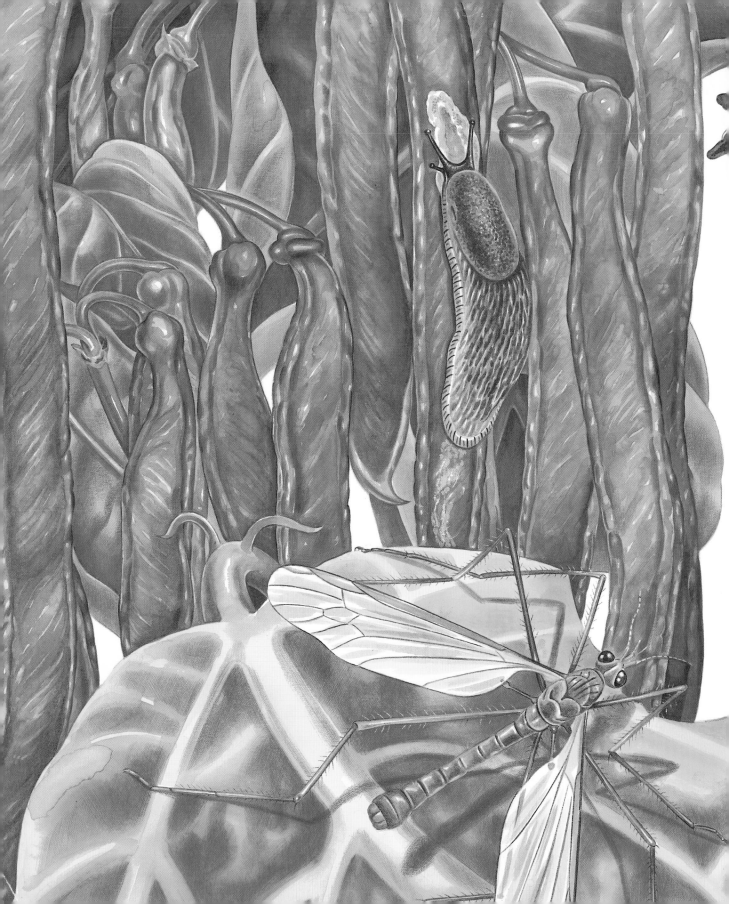

· Cycles of Life ·
Growing Things

Written and illustrated by Carolyn Scrace
Created and designed by David Salariya

W
FRANKLIN WATTS
A Division of Scholastic Inc.
NEW YORK • TORONTO • LONDON • AUCKLAND • SYDNEY
MEXICO CITY • NEW DELHI • HONG KONG
DANBURY, CONNECTICUT

Contents

Introduction 6

Digging the Hole 8

Planting the Seed 11

Germination 12

Root Hairs Grow 15

The Leaves Grow 16

Growing Up the Cane 19

The Flowers Grow 20

Pollination 23

The Beans Grow 24

Picking the Beans 27

The Bean Plant's Cycle 28

Growing Things Words 30

Index 31

Introduction

To help them grow, plants use
energy from the Sun and **minerals**
from the soil and rain.

In this book, you will learn
to grow a bean plant.
You will see what happens to
a small black and purple bean seed.
Flowers appear first. Then come
green beans that you can eat.

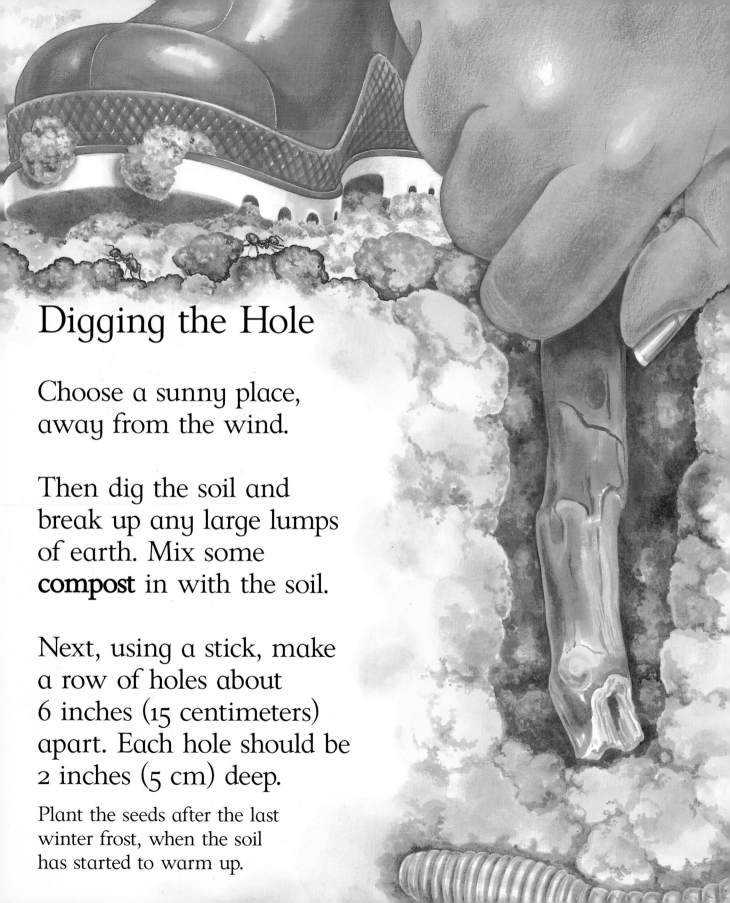

Digging the Hole

Choose a sunny place, away from the wind.

Then dig the soil and break up any large lumps of earth. Mix some **compost** in with the soil.

Next, using a stick, make a row of holes about 6 inches (15 centimeters) apart. Each hole should be 2 inches (5 cm) deep.

Plant the seeds after the last winter frost, when the soil has started to warm up.

Snail

Earthworm

Planting the Seed

Gently push one bean seed into each hole.

Cover each seed with about 1 inch (1-2 cm) of soil.

Then water the seeds.

Without plenty of water, the beans will die.

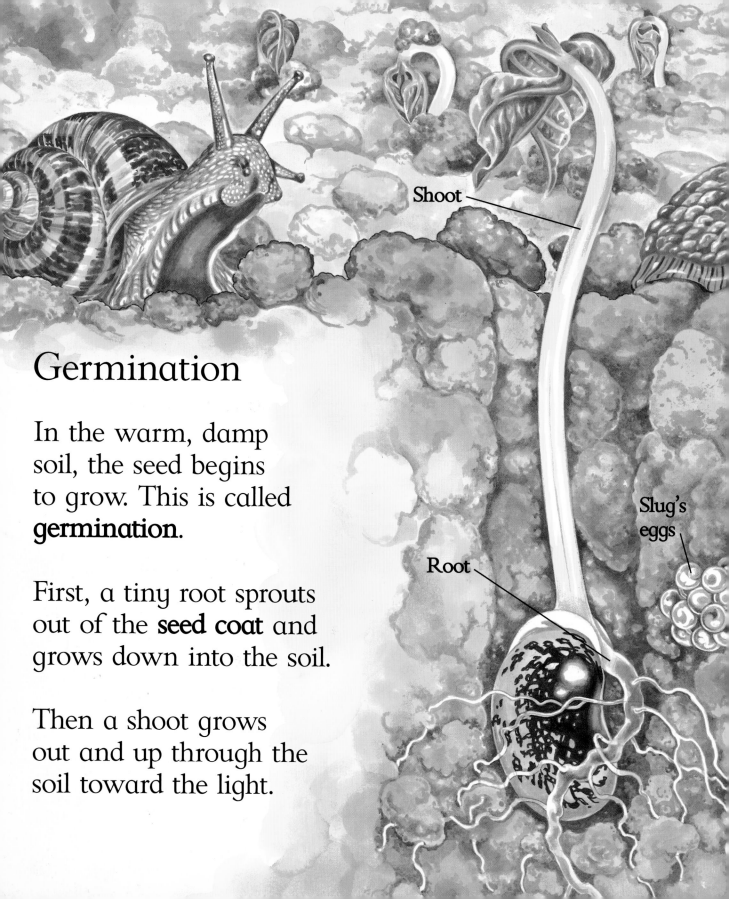

Germination

In the warm, damp soil, the seed begins to grow. This is called **germination**.

First, a tiny root sprouts out of the **seed coat** and grows down into the soil.

Then a shoot grows out and up through the soil toward the light.

Shoot

Slug's eggs

Root

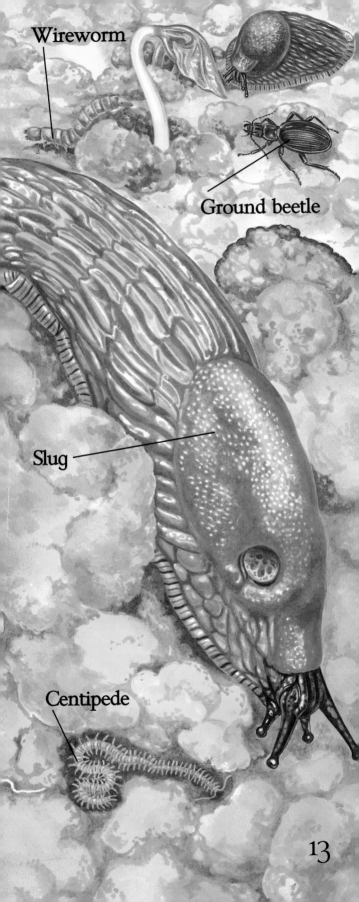

Wireworm

Ground beetle

Slug

Centipede

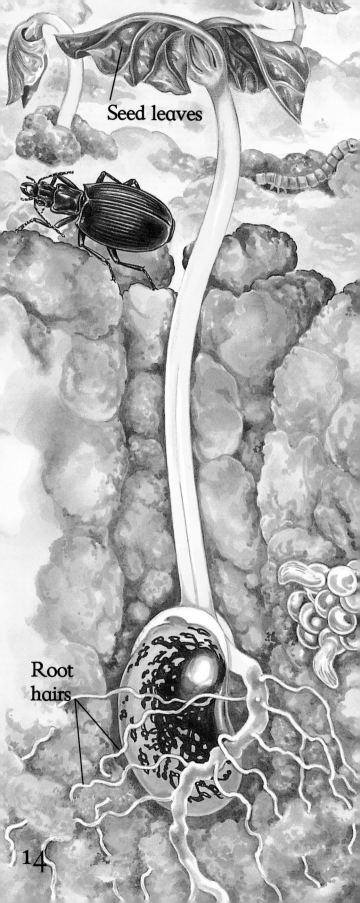

Seed leaves

Root
hairs

14

Wolf
spider

Root Hairs Grow

The new root
is covered in
fluffy **root hairs**.

Root hairs collect
minerals and
water from
the soil
to feed the
growing plant.

Soon the first
seed leaves
appear above
the ground.

15

The Leaves Grow

The young bean plant grows quickly. Its green leaves use sunlight, air, and water to make food.

Below ground, more roots grow. They take in minerals, other **nutrients**, and water from the soil.

When the plants are a few inches high, put canes in the ground to help the beans grow. Push the canes into the ground 1 foot (30 cm) apart, close to the plants. Cross the canes over at the top and tie them tightly together.

Cane

Field mouse

17

Magpie

Growing Up the Cane

The tallest shoot waves slowly around until it hits the cane. Then it begins to wind around the cane as it continues to grow.

In hot, dry weather, keep the bean plants well watered. Green beans grow counterclockwise around their canes.

19

Ladybug

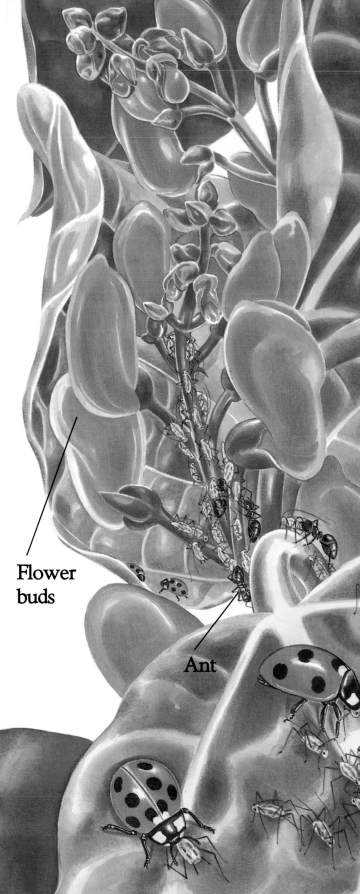

The Flowers Grow

When the bean plants are tall and strong, flower buds grow.

Aphids feed on bean plants by sucking out the **sap** from the plant stems. Aphids make **honeydew** from the sap. Ants collect the sweet honeydew from the aphids. Ladybugs eat aphids.

Flower buds

Ant

Aphid

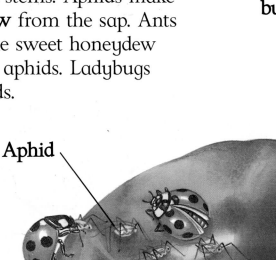

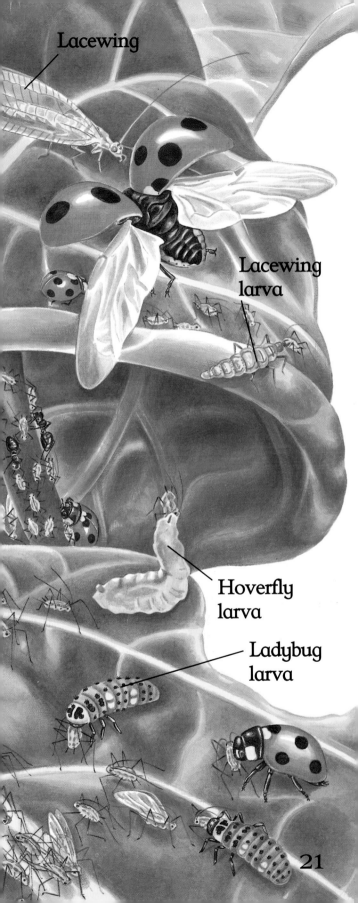

Lacewing

Lacewing larva

Hoverfly larva

Ladybug larva

21

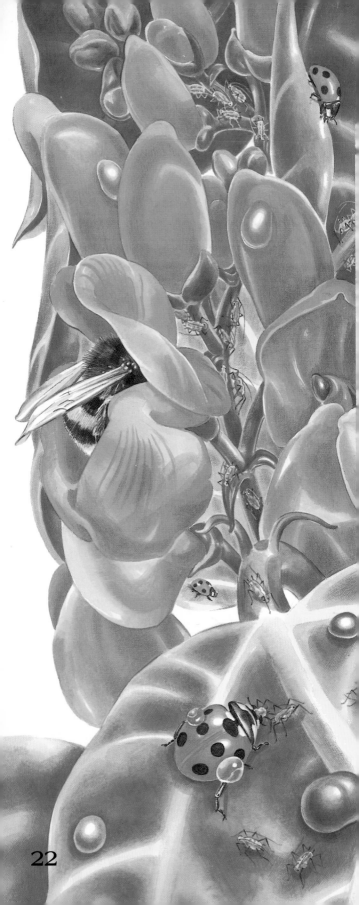

Hoverfly

Pollination

Bees fly from one plant to another. They crawl inside the flowers looking for **nectar**, and their hairy bodies get covered in **pollen**.

When bees fly to the next plant, some of the pollen from the first flower gets rubbed off onto the next flower and **fertilizes** it.

This is called **pollination**.

Bee

Stink bug

The Beans Grow

Once the flowers have been pollinated, tiny green beans begin to grow. The flowers disappear.

The beans are ready for picking about fifteen weeks after the seeds are planted.

The bean plant reaches a height of 60-80 inches (150-200 cm) when grown up a cane.

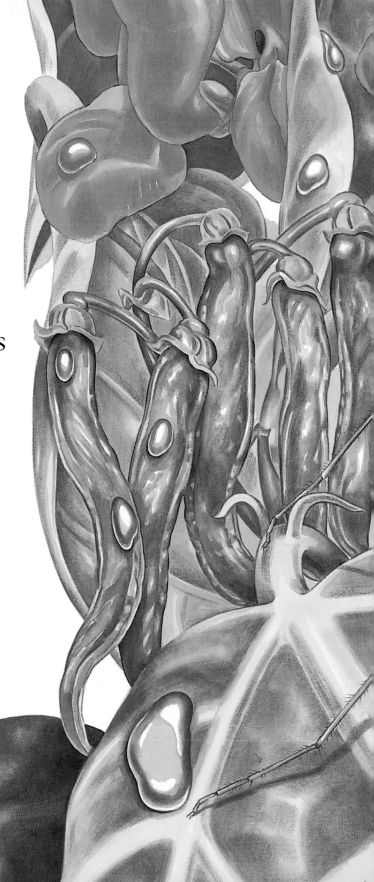

Butterfly

24

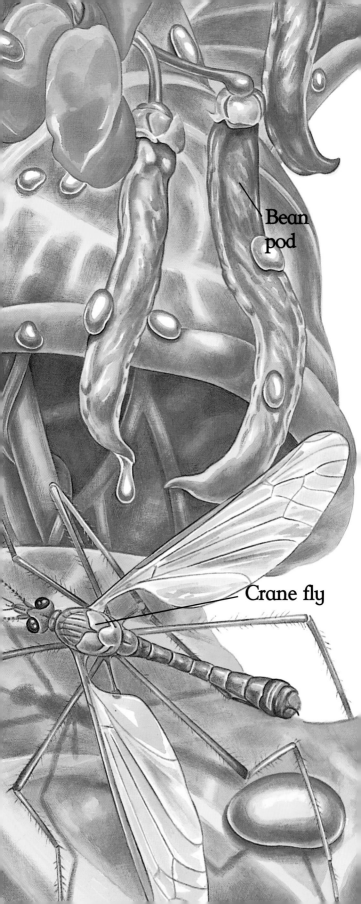

Bean pod

Crane fly

Bush cricket

Picking the Beans

The best time to pick the beans for eating is when they are about 5 inches (15 cm) long.

Keep picking the beans as they are ready to eat. The plant will continue to flower and grow more beans.

If you leave the beans for too long, they become too tough to eat.

27

The Bean Plant's Cycle

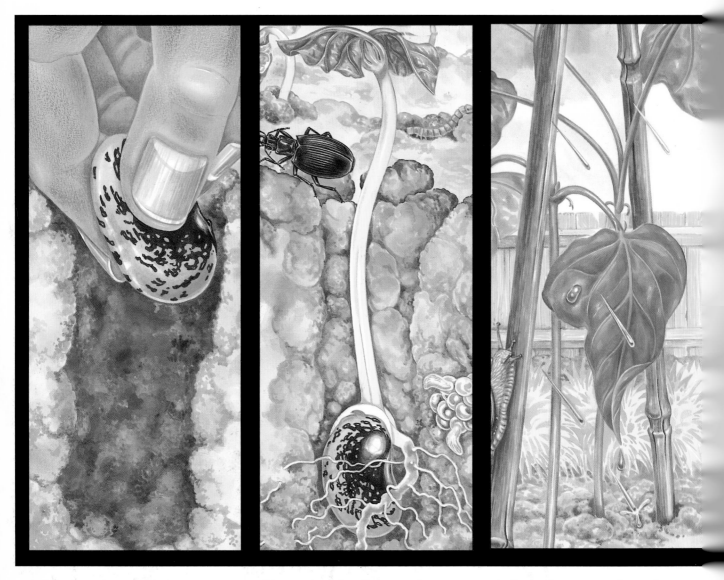

The bean seed is planted in late April or early May.

Two weeks later, the young shoot has grown up through the soil. The first seed leaves appear.

After four weeks, the plant is 15 inches (40 cm high. After ten weeks, the plant is fully grown at 3 feet (1 m) high.

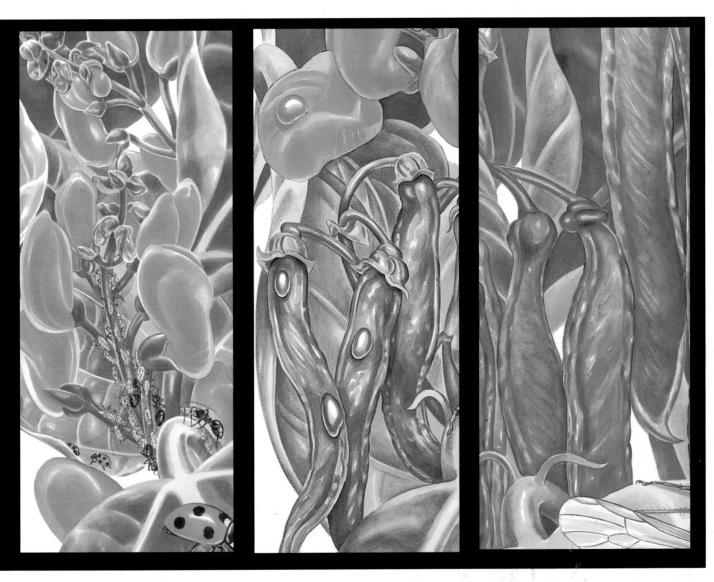

The plant starts to grow flower buds after eleven weeks.

After thirteen weeks, the first beans begin to grow.

About fifteen weeks after planting the seed, the beans are ready to be picked.

Growing Things Words

Aphid
An insect with a soft oval body, a small head, eyes, two long antennae, and a sharp beak

Bee
An insect covered in stiff black and yellow hairs. It has a stinger that it uses in defense.

Compost
Plants that have rotted and become food for growing plants

Fertilize
To join the pollen from the male part of a flower with the female part of a flower

Germination
When a seed comes to life and begins to grow

Honeydew
The sweet, sticky fluid that an aphid produces

after it has fed on sap

Ladybug
A type of beetle with a small black head, two eyes, and two short antennae

Larva
A stage in the life cycle of an insect before it grows into an adult

Minerals
Special food, found in the soil, that helps plants grow

Nectar
Sweet, sticky syrup made by flowers

Nutrients
The parts of food that help a seed or plant grow

Pod
A long, thin case that holds seeds

Pollen
The yellow dust from the male part of a flower

Pollination
When pollen is carried from the male part of a flower to the female part of a flower

Root hairs
Tiny hairs that grow out from roots

Sap
The watery juice found inside plants

Seed coat
The thick outer layer of a seed

Seed leaves
The first leaves that a plant grows from its seed

Index

A
ants 20
aphids 20, 30

B
bees 23, 30
bush cricket 27
butterfly 24

C
canes 16, 19
centipede 13
compost 8, 30
crane fly 25

D
digging 8

E
earthworm 9, 11
energy 6

F
field mouse 16
flowers 6, 20, 23, 24, 29, 30
frost 8

G
germination 12, 30
green beans 6, 24, 25, 27, 29
ground beetle 13

H
honeydew 20, 30
hoverfly 23

L
lacewing 21
larva 21, 30
ladybug 20, 30
leaves 16

M
magpie 17
minerals 6, 15, 16, 30

N
nectar 23, 30
nutrients 16, 30

P
planting 11, 24, 28, 29, 30
pod 25, 30

pollen 23
pollination 23, 24, 30

R
rain 6
root 12, 15, 16, 30
root hairs 14, 15, 30

S
sap 20, 30
seed 6, 8, 11, 10, 12, 24, 27, 28, 30
seed coat 12, 30
seed leaves 14, 15, 28, 30
shoot 12, 28
slug 13
snail 11
soil 6, 8, 11, 12, 15, 16, 28, 30
stink bug 23
Sun 6, 16

W
water 15, 16
winter 8
wireworm 13
wolf spider 15

Language Consultant:
Betty Root

Natural History Consultant:
Dr. Gerald Legg

Editors:
Karen Barker Smith
Stephanie Cole

Created, designed and produced by
The Salariya Book Company Ltd
Book House
25 Marlborough Place
Brighton BN1 1UB

Visit the Salariya Book Company at
www.salariya.com

Published in 2002 by Franklin Watts
A Division of Scholastic Inc.
90 Sherman Turnpike
Danbury, CT 06816

A catalog record for this title is available from
the Library of Congress.

ISBN 0-531-14659-6 (Lib. Bdg.)
ISBN 0-531-14841-6 (Pbk.)

Printed in China.